THIS JOURNAL BELONGS TO:

GW01157878

Printed in Poland
by Amazon Fulfillment
Poland Sp. z o.o., Wrocław

51055542R00069